THIS BOOK BELONGS TO:
....
....
....

Happy holidays everyone!

HODDER CHILDREN'S BOOKS

First published in Great Britain in 2025
by Hodder & Stoughton

1 3 5 7 9 10 8 6 4 2

Text and illustrations copyright © Matt Carr, 2025

The moral rights of the author-illustrator
have been asserted.

All rights reserved.

A CIP catalogue record for this book
is available from the British Library.

ISBN 978 1 444 95215 5

Printed and bound in China

Hodder Children's Books
An imprint of Hachette Children's Group
Part of Hodder & Stoughton Limited
Carmelite House, 50 Victoria Embankment,
London, EC4Y 0DZ

An Hachette UK Company
www.hachette.co.uk
www.hachettechildrens.co.uk

The authorised representative in the EEA
is Hachette Ireland, 8 Castlecourt Centre,
Dublin 15, D15 XTP3, Ireland (email: info@hbgi.ie)

BAUBLE in TROUBLE

Matt Carr

Hodder Children's Books

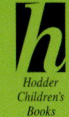

'Twas the night before Christmas,
the children were sleeping,

when up in the loft
came the faint sound of weeping...

Then she spied a small window,
felt a breeze on her face.
"Come on, Beryl," she said.
"Let's get out of this place!"

But outside the wind caught her.
Beryl started to fall.
She rolled and turned into
A GIANT SNOWBALL!

When she ran out of roof,
Beryl **JUST** couldn't stop!
She sped off the edge
down a very long...

But Beryl thought fast,
swinging off some lights quickly...

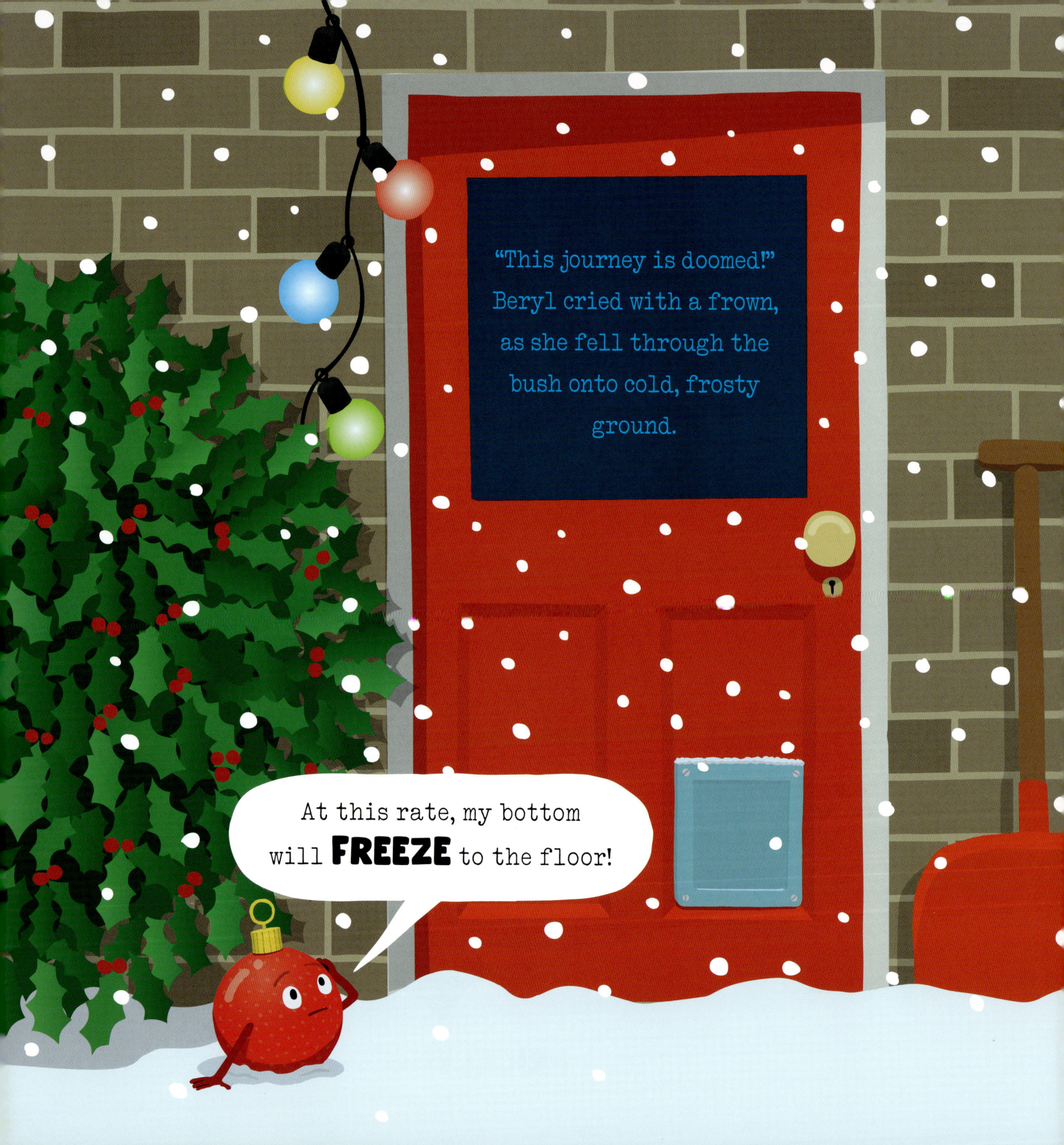

Inside, safe and warm,
but with some way to go,
Beryl aimed for the tree,
with its cosy, warm glow.

And with no time to lose, Beryl started to roll!

But the room was so dark, she spun out of control.

The playful puss batted Beryl about,

'til a **NOISE** from the chimney made Kitty run out.

First one boot,
then two,
then a loud

HO, HO, HO!

as Beryl lay still
in the fireplace below.

Poor Beryl!
Already so tired,
bruised and battered.
One step from
that boot and
Christmas is
SHATTERED!

With the last of her strength, Beryl rolled from the DANGER...

...and she caught the eye of a jolly old stranger.

"I think," Santa said, "this is where you should be." And gently he placed her back up in the tree.

"My Christmas is saved! Thank you, Santa!" said Beryl.

At **LAST**, she had made it — through snow, sprouts and peril.